Early Preventio

THE HYENA WHO LOST HER LAUGH

A Story About Changing Your Negative Thinking

by Jessica Lamb-Shapiro
illustrated by Denise Gilgannon

1-800-962-1141

THE HYENA WHO LOST HER LAUGH

A Story About Changing Your Negative Thinking

by Jessica Lamb-Shapiro
illustrated by Denise Gilgannon

Childswork/Childsplay publishes products for mental health professionals, teachers and parents who wish to help children with their developmental, social and emotional growth.
For questions and comments, call 1-800-962-1141.

2 kyline Drive, Suite 101
Hawthorne, NY 10532

Printed in the United States of America

ISBN 10: 1-58815-005-4
ISBN 13: 978-1-58815-005-9

Product # 367082

Introduction

The incidence of depression in children and adolescents has increased more than tenfold in the last fifty years, and it is being diagnosed at a much earlier age. If left untreated, depression can become a chronic, lifelong, even life-threatening, problem. But only a fraction of the children who show signs of depression are receiving the appropriate treatment.

Fortunately, we have discovered depression can be prevented through fairly simple techniques, particularly when these techniques are used when children are young. This book, like the others in the Childswork/Childsplay™ Early Prevention Series, teaches children a new way to cope with difficult feelings, which has been shown to be effective in clinical research (The Optimistic Child by Martin Seligman, Houghton-Mifflin, Boston, MA, 1995).

The technique demonstrated in this story is referred to as "optimistic thinking." Over one thousand studies, involving more than a half million children, teens and adults, show optimistic people are less frequently depressed, more successful in school and on the job, and physically healthier than pessimistic people. More importantly, these studies conclude an optimistic thinking style can be taught to children who are not born with an optimistic disposition.

In this story Hillary the Hyena makes a series of mistakes and begins to feel she cannot do anything right. Pessimistic people believe they will keep making mistakes and their mistakes will occur in every area of their life. This pattern of thinking then leads them to look for negative events and to react to these events from a fatalistic worldview.

But the adults in Hillary's life teach her that mistakes are isolated events. Mistakes are usually not very important and can be corrected with additional effort. This positive view of the world and oneself is characteristic of optimistic and successful people.

Of course, one storybook cannot change the way a child thinks. If you know a child who is negative and self-deprecating, look carefully at that child's behaviors and how he/she handles life's problems. If you are concerned, consult a professional counselor, especially if there is a family history of depression. Remember, early intervention is always the best way to avoid serious problems.

Lawrence E. Shapiro, Ph.D.
June 2000

Activity Sheet

The Childswork/Childsplay Early Prevention Series is designed to help young children learn about common emotional problems and acquire the skills that can prevent early signs of trouble from becoming serious symptoms. In *The Hyena Who Lost Her Laugh*, Hillary the Hyena learns that when she is more optimistic and realistic in her thinking, she feels better and has more success. She also has more fun with her friends.

You can reinforce importance of optimistic and realistic thinking by using the Hillary the Hyena doll in a variety of activities, such as the ones below.

Talking Back to Negative Thinking

Researchers have found out that some children are naturally more prone to negative, self-deprecating thoughts, making them more at risk for depression and other mental health problems. These children can be taught to identify their negative thoughts and to "talk back," changing negative thoughts into positive ones. You can try this with the Hillary doll. Begin by taking the doll and making a negative statement, and then having the doll change it to a realistic, positive one. For example:

> Say: "I'll never learn how be a good speller."
> Hillary says: "The more I practice, the better I will be. There are many ways to help me learn good spelling."

It is important to make the positive statements realistic ones that don't reflect a "Pollyanna" attitude. The positive statement should show the child how to achieve more success. After several examples, have the child take the Hillary doll and rebut your negative statements with realistic, positive ones.

Role Play

Act out the story from the book. The adult should narrate the story and take the role of the other characters, but let the child take the doll and act out her character. If the child is a nonreader, the adult can simply tell the child what to say.

Make Up Plays with Hillary and Other Dolls

It is not easy for many young children to learn to be positive. It takes a great deal of practice. You can encourage children to adopt this new way of thinking by making up plays with them, using the Hillary doll and other figures that the child chooses to play with. Let the child suggest the plot of the story; it will likely reflect problems that he is currently facing. Guide the child to come up with a positive ending, like the one in the storybook.

You may want to make a videotape of the dolls acting out the story, which the child can then watch. A basic rule to remember is that the more a child sees a positive image of himself conquering a problem behavior, the more he will be able to cope with real situations.

Use the Hillary the Hyena Doll as a Reminder

Young children often attribute magical powers to their toys. A child may want to have the Hillary doll as a reminder that she can think more positively about herself and her world.

Hillary had not gone outside all day. She sat meekly at her bedroom desk, with her head in her hands, thinking and worrying.

HILLARY

Hillary's mom walked in, and Hillary didn't even look at her.

"Hillary, come out of your room, please. Come down to the kitchen, and we'll have some cookies and a chat."

"No, thanks, Mom. I don't feel like it."

Earlier that day, Hillary's friends had come over to see her.

"Hey, Hillary, come on out and play with us," her best friend Harry shouted. "We're chasing birds."

"No, thanks, Guys. I don't feel like it," Hillary replied, without any of her usual enthusiasm.

Hillary was popular among the other hyenas because she laughed so much. She had a very wonderful laugh that sounded like parrots squawking, dishes breaking, and bells ringing, all at once.

All the hyenas knew when Hillary was laughing.

But her friends hadn't heard that laugh for weeks.

11

Later, when Hillary's brother Franklin came into her bedroom to talk, Hillary didn't smile. She didn't even seem to care he was there. She just wanted to fall asleep.

Franklin made funny faces, and Hillary yawned.

He stood on his head, and Hillary sighed.

He even tried to tickle her with feathers, but she only looked annoyed.

"Come on, Hillary, I know there's a laugh in you. Let me hear it," he begged.

"Not now, Franklin. I'm not in the mood," Hillary said.

Hillary didn't feel interested in any of the activities she used to like, and she didn't really know why.

When her dad came home, he went into her bedroom to speak with her.

"What's wrong, Hillary?" he asked.

Hillary only sighed and said, "Everything! It started last week. Mrs. Toothen told us we were going to have a spelling test. I was excited because I'm really good at spelling. At least I thought I was. I studied a lot of words, but I still got a 'D' on the test. I guess I'm just stupid."

Hillary got even more upset as she continued to tell her dad about the events of the past week.

"When my friends and I were playing kickball after school, I dropped the ball and our team lost the tournament. Now all my friends hate me. I can't do anything right. I'm no good in school, and I'm no good at sports."

"It sounds like you have had a rough week," Hillary's dad said, as he pulled up a stool to sit next to her.

"It's been terrible!" Hillary agreed.

"Maybe you should try looking at it all in a different way," he said. "You said you were good at spelling, but maybe the words on the spelling test were different than the ones you studied. Maybe you just need to study harder next time."

Then Hillary's dad put his arm around her shoulders.

"And as far as the kickball game goes, it sounds like you just made a mistake. Everyone makes a mistake sometimes," Hillary's dad explained.

"You just don't understand," Hillary said softly, as she began to cry.

HILLARY

"I understand it felt awful to get a 'D,' " said Hillary's dad. "And when you made a mistake and your team lost the tournament, I know you felt responsible. But do you really think your friends hate you? Would you hate one of your teammates if she had made the same mistake?"

"I guess not," said Hillary.

HILLARY
D

"Sometimes if you think about things differently, you feel differently," Hillary's dad said. "I want you to try to think more positively from now on. If you catch yourself having a negative thought and feeling sorry for yourself, I want you to change that thought into a positive one. I think you'll find a positive attitude goes a long way to solving most problems."

Hillary's dad patted her on the head and left her alone to think about what he had said.

Hillary felt a little better, but she hardly felt like laughing.

"It won't make any difference. I'm still a failure, but I'll give it a try," Hillary thought to herself.

Hillary got up from her chair, determined to try.

The next day Hillary had a drum lesson.

She played well for the first two pages of music, but on the third page she made a mistake. She dropped her drumsticks and sank to the floor.

"I'm terrible at drumming," she complained to her drum teacher. "I don't know why my parents are making me learn an instrument. Don't they know I'm not good at anything?"

LET'S MAKE
Music

Mr. Bailey, her drum teacher, stared at her in bewilderment.

"You just made one mistake, Hillary," he said. "Making a mistake doesn't mean you're bad at something. It just means you need to try again, a little harder."

LET'S MAKE
Music

Hillary was feeling like things were hopeless, but she thought about what her dad had said. It sounded a lot like what Mr. Bailey had just told her.

"Maybe I'm not so terrible at drumming, and maybe I did just make a mistake," she thought.

Hillary picked up her drumsticks once again and tried a little harder. She did make another mistake, but it wasn't until the fourth page of music, and then she just kept going.

"It's just a mistake, and it's not the same one as before, so I did learn something," she thought to herself.

LET'S MAKE
Music

By the end of the lesson, she could play the piece perfectly. After her drum lesson Hillary was feeling much better. She really loved playing the drums.

But then she heard a voice inside her say something that made her feel bad again.

The voice said, "Just because you finally got one piece right doesn't mean you're not stupid. You'll probably mess up the next time. You never do anything right."

YOU NEVER DO ANYTHING RIGHT!

Hillary started to feel upset again.

But then she thought, "What if it's the other way around? What if I am smart, but sometimes I still can't get things right? Does that mean I should give up? No way!"

Hillary started to feel better again once she thought about it differently.

The next day Hillary went to her friend Janet's house. Janet was using paper and glue and crayons and scissors to make a rocket ship.

"Janet, you're so good at making things. I'd never be able to come up with an idea for making paper rocket ships like you did," Hillary said.

"I bet you could make one just like mine. Just watch how I do it, grab some supplies, and try," Janet said.

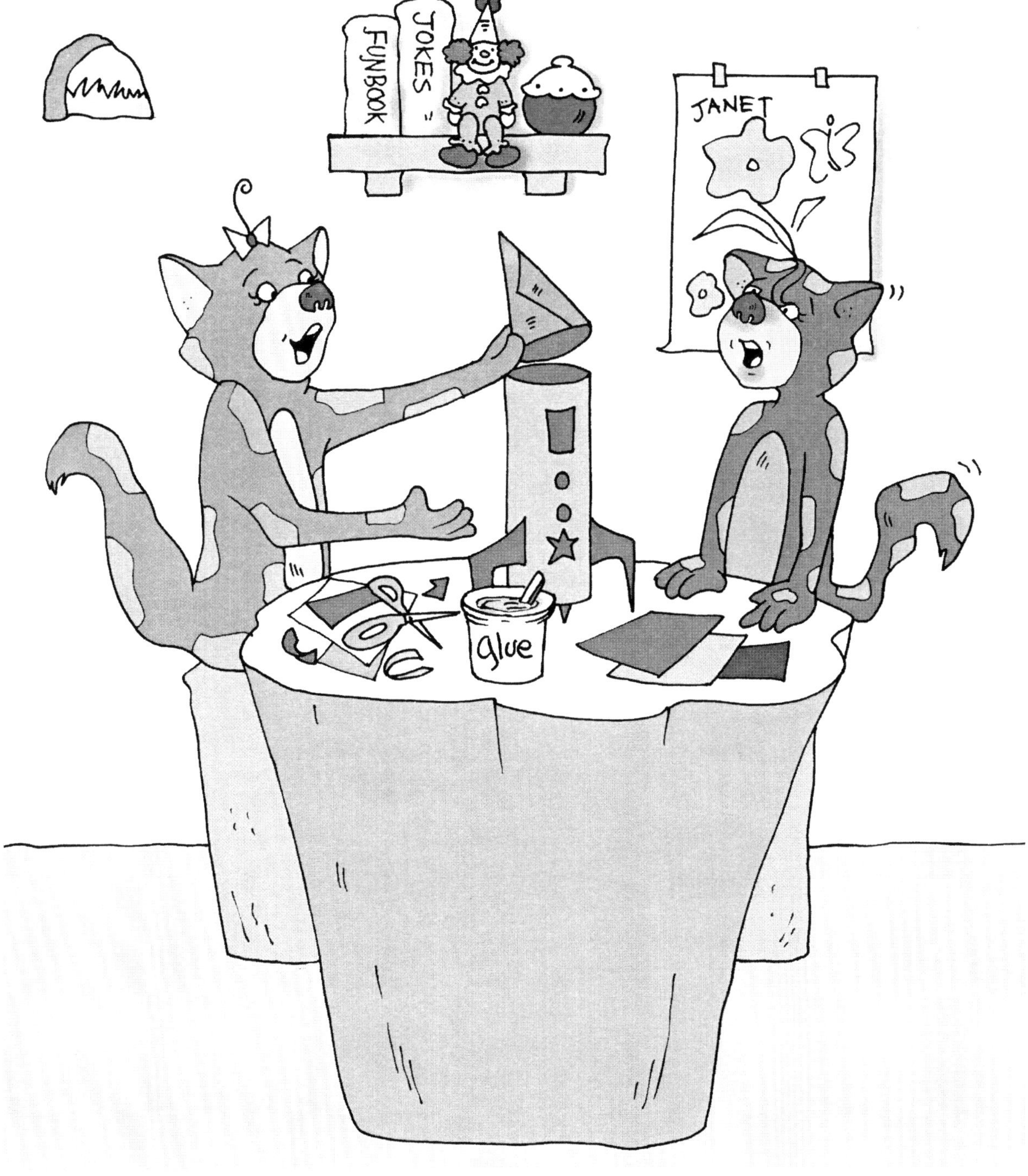
FUNBOOK
JOKES
JANET
glue

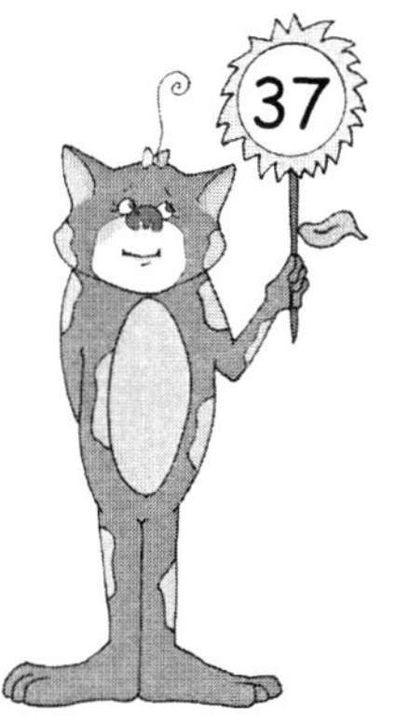

Hillary sat down next to Janet and started working, paying close attention to what Janet was doing.

But no matter what Hillary did, her rocket ship didn't look anything like Janet's. It didn't look like anything at all!

"It's no use, Janet. I'm using the same stuff as you, and I think I'm doing what you're doing, but I'm just making a big mess of it all," Hillary said, holding up a poor imitation of Janet's rocket ship.

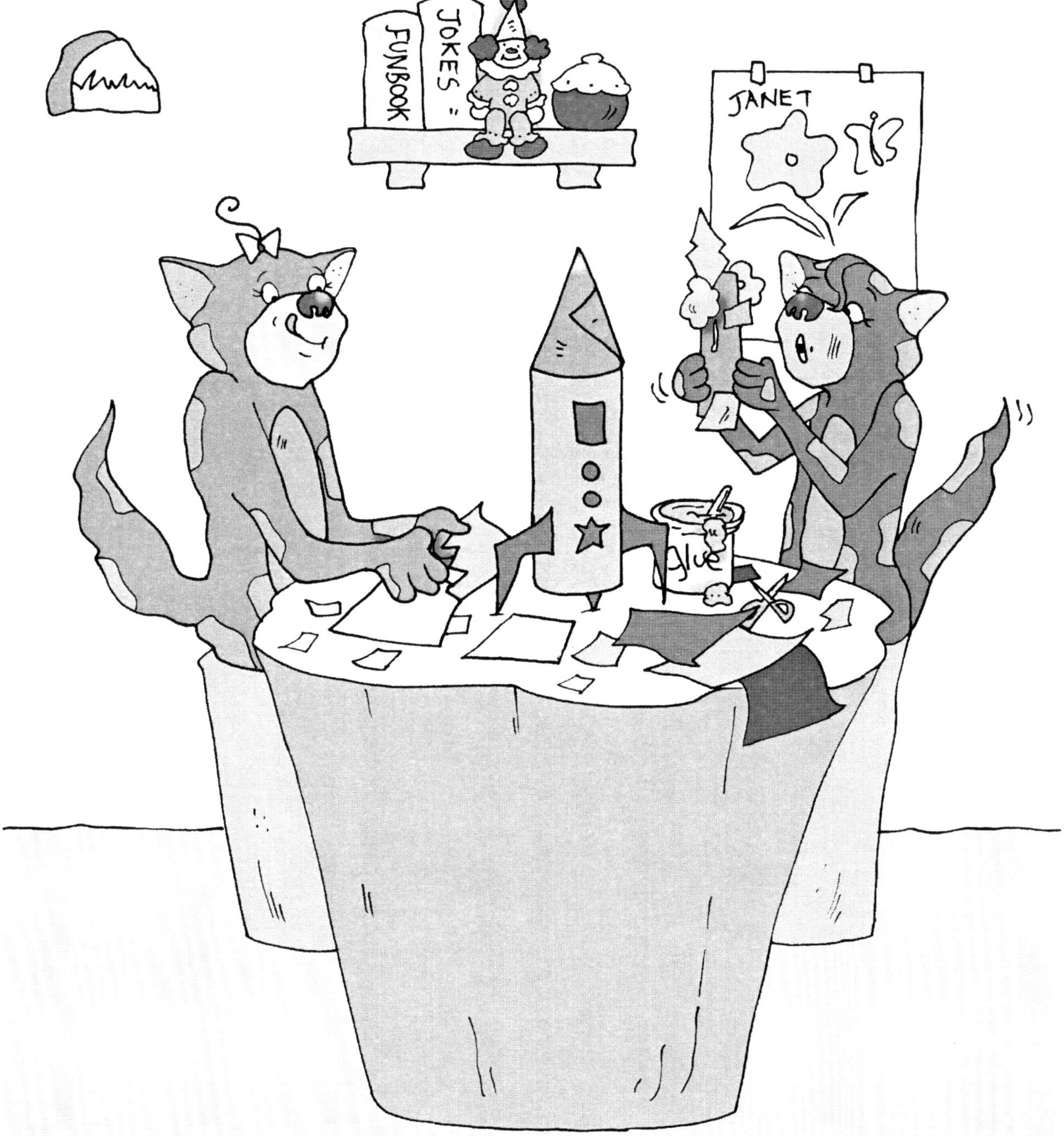
FUNBOOK
JOKES
JANET
Glue

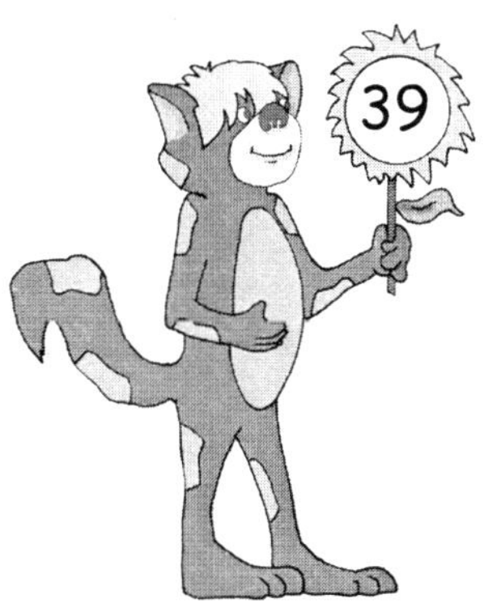

Suddenly the room was filled with the sound of paper tearing. Hillary was so totally frustrated and sad, she just tore her work into a zillion pieces.

"Why did you do that?" Janet asked.

"Mine was stinky," said Hillary. "It wasn't as good as yours. No matter how hard I try, I could never make things like you do."

41

"That's not true," said Janet. "My first rocket ship looked worse than yours. This was your first one, Hillary. When you've made as many as I have, yours will look great, too."

"Really?" asked Hillary.

"Really," said Janet.

43

Later that afternoon when Hillary returned home from Janet's house, Hillary's mom was busy preparing dinner.

"Hillary, would you give me a hand? Would you bake a cake for dessert tonight?" her mom asked.

"Sure, Mom. You know I love to bake, and I'm really hungry. A cake after dinner sounds great to me!" Hillary said.

Hillary measured out the ingredients into a large bowl, one by one, the flour and the sugar and all the rest.

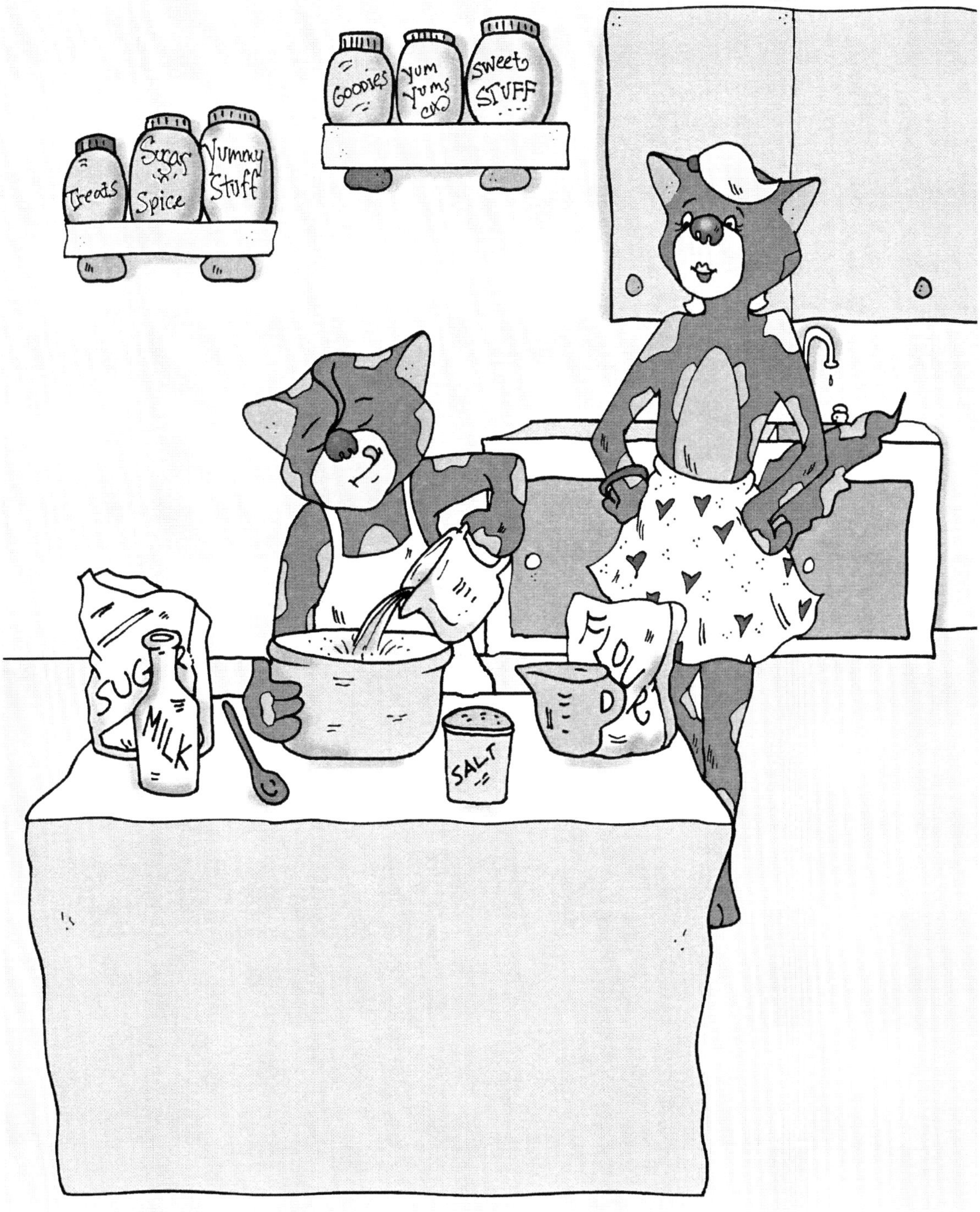
Treats
Sugar
Spice
Yummy Stuff
Goodies
Yum Yums
Sweet STUFF
MILK
SALT

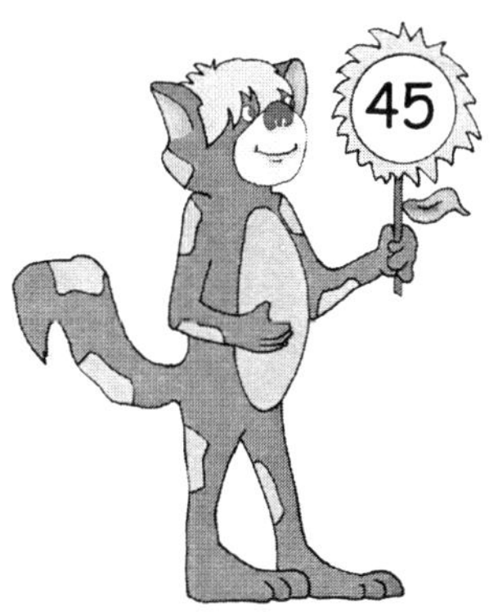

After dinner everyone was eager to taste Hillary's cake. It looked almost too good to eat.

Hillary's dad took a big bite and said, "This is going to taste so..."

Then he gasped, with a strange look on his face, and tried to swallow the cake.

Hillary took a big bite herself and knew immediately what the problem was. She had added much too much salt. It felt gritty in the mouth, and it burned all the way down!

Hillary's eyes filled with tears. She had ruined dinner.

"Don't cry," said Franklin. "The icing is really great!"

"Don't cry," said Hillary's mom. "Franklin's right. The icing is really, really great!"

"Don't cry," said Hillary's dad. "This is the best icing I've ever tasted!"

Then, to everyone's surprise, Hillary stood up and laughed.

Her laugh shook the whole room. It made the forks fall off the table. Even the light above the table started swinging.

"I put too much salt in the cake. It's terrible," Hillary laughed. "That's the yuckiest cake I ever tasted!"

And Hillary laughed even harder.

And her family laughed, too.

But no one laughed quite like Hillary.

When everyone finally stopped laughing, Hillary asked, "Can I make another cake after dinner, Mom?"

Hillary's mom smiled. "Of course, you can. If at first you don't succeed, try, try again."

"That's just what I'll do," Hillary thought, as she began laughing again.

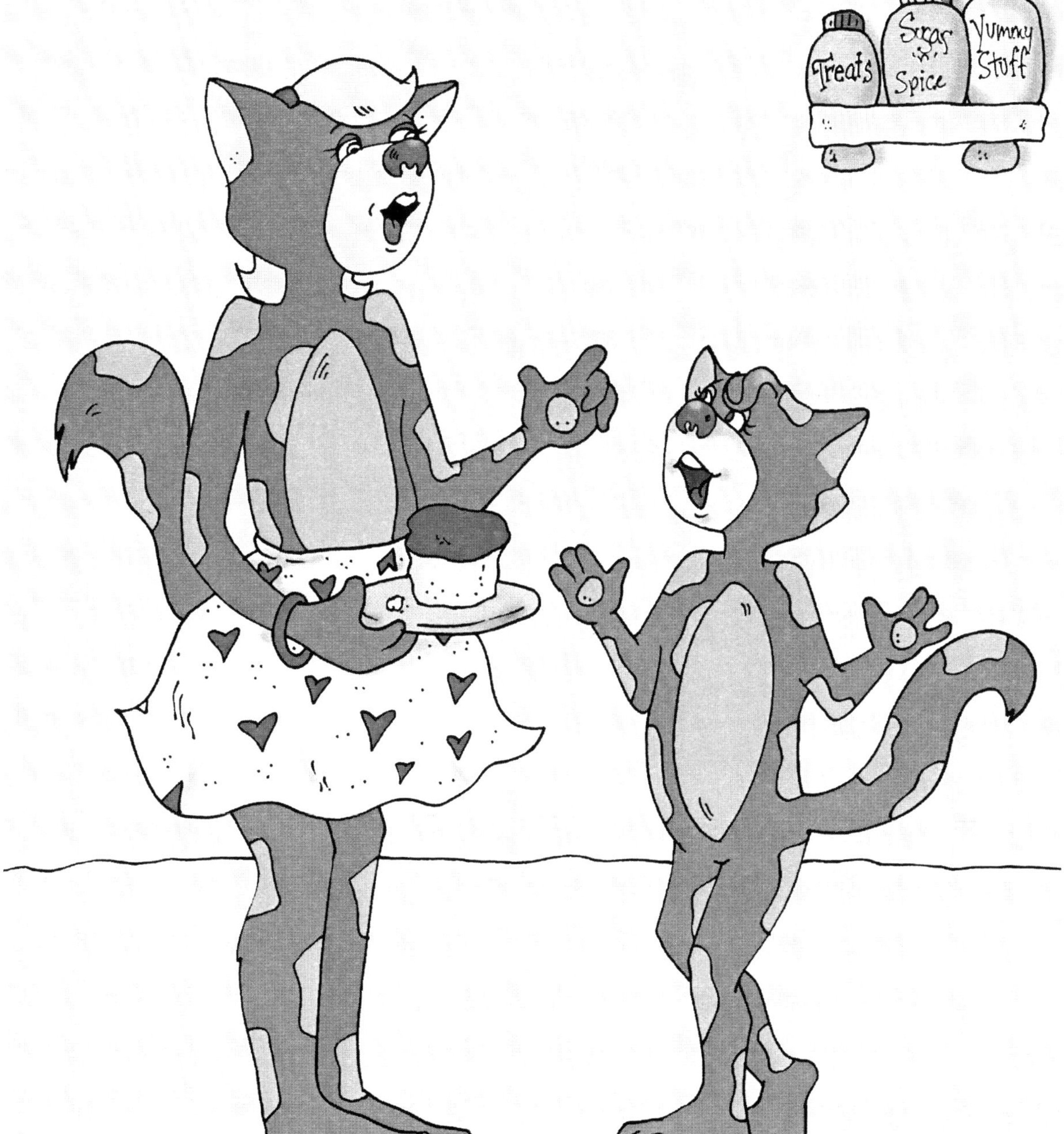
Treats
Sugar 'n' Spice
Yummy Stuff

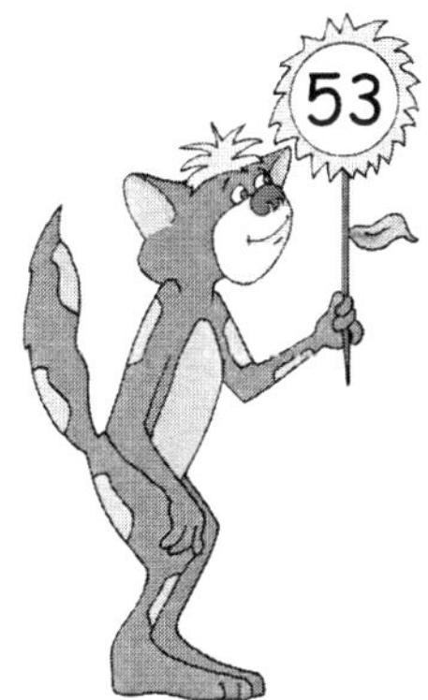